Keep Me Faithful

Keep Me Faithful

Prayer-poems on the life of faith

Ruth Harms Calkin

LIVING BOOKS
Tyndale House Publishers, Inc.
Wheaton, Illinois

With deep gratitude
to our treasured friends
Happi and Roger
So often used of God
to make beautiful things happen!

Contents

Acknowledgments

The following poems first appeared in other Tyndale books:

"Both," "The Difference," "A Doubt," "Forgiving Lord," "Gentle Whisper," "I Hope So, Too," "I Wonder Why?" "Inconsistency," "It's Bound to Be Good," "The Majestic Name," and "A Quiet Tongue" were previously published in *Lord, Could You Hurry a Little?* (1983).

"Accept—Expect," "Every Valley Exalted," "Forgive My Critical Attitude," "I Am Sure of You," "I Know You Best," "I Really Knew," "Immediately," "Lost Argument," "Moment by Moment," "Never Too Late," "One Stupendous Thing," "The Prayer," "Relentless," and "Soul Struggle" were previously published in *Lord, Don't You Love Me Anymore?* (1988).

"Authentic," "Communication Breakdown," "The Deliberate No," "Frustrated Desires," "Grandfather," "Heaven's Joy," "I Plead with You," "Settled Decision," "Small Bit of Heaven," "So Ashamed," "Telltale Signs," and "When I Cannot Utter a Word" were previously published in *Lord, I Just Keep Running in Circles* (1988).

"Beginning," "Factual," "I Keep Running Back to You," "Loud and Clear," "Marvelous Moments," "Mistaken Values," "My Life Is Richer," "New Bible," "Trusting," "What More Could a Mother Ask?" "Why in the World?" and "You Name the Stars" were previously published in *Lord, I Keep Running Back to You* (1983).

"Always Thinking," "Autumn Glow," "Burning Bushes," "Explanation," "The Great Contrast," "I Sing in the Rain," "I Trust," "It Keeps Happening," "Listen Trustingly," "Painfully New," "Part of the Gift" (originally titled "The Gift"), "Spiritual Mathematics," and "What Would Happen?" were previously published in *Lord, It Keeps Happening . . . and Happening* (1984).

A Life
with Others

The Sand Castle

About age four, and small as four
She planned (as I watched)
Her castle in the sand.
It took but a short time of building
Before she noticed that water crept up
Constantly destroying her creation.

Now that's just enough
She said to the swelling tide.
In no way did she hide her impatience.

No more water, please!
I said please, didn't I?
But on came the tide
Ignoring her completely
Destroying her foundation
As fast as she was digging.

In a tone most stern
And with eyes flashing
She tried once more.
I told you that is quite enough.
Don't you ever listen?
I don't need any more cold water.
I really *mean* it!

Little age-four builder
Trying to control
A billion-year-old sea.
I laughed, and then I thought
Oh, oh, could that be me?

Special Friendship

Lord, this morning I thank You
With renewed appreciation
For the exquisite gift of friendship
And for my special friend
With her happy heart
Whose life is so intertwined with mine.

Thank You for her healthy optimism
Her enduring values
Her childlike trust in You.
Thank You for her creativity
So expansively shared.
Thank You for her direct honesty
Her radiant enthusiasm
Her refreshing freedom.
Thank You for her listening ear
Her ready response to needs.
Thank You for the way
Our thoughts walk arm in arm.
Thank You that together
We can be utterly ourselves
Without pretense—
Without fear.
Thank You that we can pray together
Laugh and cry together
Cushion defeats
And applaud victories together.

I Really Knew

I have discovered, Lord
That some hospital visitors
Are extremely insensitive to timing.
I remember the woman who came to visit
When my husband was at his very worst.
The doctor had just said to me
"We are puzzled. Your husband is very ill
And we have not found the cause of his
    illness."
The woman listened with a broad smile.
She was in exuberant health.
Never had she been a patient in a hospital.
I wondered as I looked at her
If she had ever suffered great pain.
"Remember," she said triumphantly
"God never gives us more than we can
    bear!"
Lord, I knew what she said was true.
I really *knew.*
And yet at that moment, dear God
I would so much rather have heard it from
    You.

We cross in front of the halting traffic
And I hear his whispered *"Thank you."*

My heart throbs with poignant memories
With love
With deep gratitude
As we walk together—
My dad and I.

Lord, every path I've walked with Dad
Has led to You.

While She Waits

Lord
They hadn't wanted it like this—
Nor had they anticipated
The sudden drastic change.
Faithfully, with infinite patience
He'd taken care of her
Day by day, year after year.
He'd fixed her meals
Helped her into her clothes—
Even combed her thinning hair.
He'd read to her by the hour
Written short notes
And fluffed the pillows
Behind her aching back.
Theirs was a beautiful devotion
And now he's gone
And she is so desperately lonely.
Today between choking sobs
She told me how she longed to join him.
Surely You understand, dear Lord.
Take her with You soon, I pray.
Give her her heart's desire.
And while she waits
May those of us who love her
Do what we can to make the lonely hours
A little less painful.

The years pass so swiftly.
One of these days, without any doubt
Jesus will be coming, and I will be going.
All my cherished possessions will remain.
I'll take nothing with me
But an overwhelming abundance of love.
At times I think of it wonderingly
When I lie in the quiet stillness.

Only once did I awaken my husband.
I needed his gentle assurance.
I remember that he said
"It will happen to us both, my darling.
But one thing we know—
Jesus will be there, so it's bound to be good."

I'm not counting years, I'm *living* them.
Through all Eternity I'll go right on *living*.
One thing I know, dear Lord:
You'll be there, so it's bound to be good!

"Mom: You're like a personal rainbow
After a storm.
Thanks—and a whole bunch of love."

Dear Lord
What more could a mother ask?

Give her a fresh, breathtaking glimpse
Of the joy that can be hers
When she is totally occupied with You.

I Weep with the Joy of My Love

Lord, I weep with the joy
Of my love for him. . . .

He seldom walks in
He darts—
Arms outstretched
For a vigorous hug.
He's seldom alone
A Little Leaguer trails him—
Three feet tall
Four teeth missing.
(A dog named Tagalong tags along.)
He's seldom hungry
He's starved.
"David and me would like some cookies."
"You mean 'David and I.'"
"Sure, Mom, you too."
He seldom runs out to play
He races.
At the table he seldom swallows
He inhales.
At bedtime he seldom prays
He climbs up on God's lap
And in a manner most beautiful
He whispers his own private secrets.
He seldom asks
He thanks—
For this and this
And especially for this. . . .

The Stab

Lord, I was thoroughly exasperated
With our newsboy.
Three times my husband requested
That he throw our paper on the porch
But there it was again—
In the middle of the lawn.
I dashed out the door
To vent my irritation.
In no uncertain terms I made it clear
That such negligence was inexcusable
That he'd never hold a responsible job
That most boys his age . . .

Well, Lord, You heard me—
Fury flying.
He looked at me curiously
Trying to put it together.
Then suddenly the dawn:
"Hey, I know you—
You're my sister's Sunday school teacher.
You talk about God and love and stuff."
Lord, I'm stabbed with shame.
Forgive me
Recreate me
Until my life on Monday
Authentically reflects
What I teach on Sunday.

Frustrated Desires

All day long, dear Lord
Her haunting words
Have swept through my aching heart.
"Frustrated desires . . ."
Together we stood at the card rack
Looking at birthday cards.
Wanting to be friendly
I said nonchalantly
"It's difficult to choose
When they're all so beautiful."
She looked toward me pensively.
"My husband died three months ago.
We always gave each other
Beautiful cards.
Today is his birthday.
I wish I could give him
The whole rack."
Pushing back the tears
She said half-apologetically
"I'm sorry, I didn't mean
To trouble you
With my frustrated desires."

I cannot comfort her, Lord.
I don't even know her name.
She left the store so quickly.
But not for a single moment
Is she lost to You.
Wherever she is right now

Explanation

Just this week
I read a newspaper account
Of a thirteen-year-old boy
Who saved his brother's life
By driving him to a hospital
In his father's car.
Never having driven before
His explanation was simple:
"I just did what I saw my father do."

O dear God
Please empower me to bring life
To a sick, wounded world
With the simple explanation:
"I do what my Father does."

What Would Happen?

Lord, thank You for the dear woman
Who long ago said to my preacher-father
"Every morning at six o'clock
I fervently pray for you."

God, I wonder . . .
What would happen in churches
Across the land
If every morning at six o'clock
A dozen faithful members
In every church
Prayed fervently for their pastor.

My dad:
Once virile, strong, alert
Once intellectually stimulating
A scholar, a teacher
Who dreamed noble dreams
And planned lavish schemes.
From the pulpit he challenged youths
Comforted the oppressed
And boldly presented the claims of Christ.
He loved and laughed and lived.

Forgive my glibness, Lord
My indifference
My condescension.
Create in me a deep compassion
A tender empathy.
In every ward and room
May I see a dad
A mother
A person of infinite worth.
Above all
With every gentle touch
May I see You.

Soul Struggle

Her uncontrollable sobs know no respite.
"What is wrong with me"
She stammers convulsively
"That love has passed me by?
Am I so ugly, so stupidly plain?
Am I some kind of an oddity?
Doesn't God love me anymore?"

Lord, there are times when she hides
Behind a sophisticated facade
But today she is not pretending.
In her deep loneliness
There are no words to comfort her.
You alone can release her
From her shadowy world.
You alone can break the bleakness
And produce the firm conviction
Of Your measureless love.
Lord, my part in her soul's struggle
Is to reach for her hand.
Your part is to reach for her heart.

Busy Busy Busy

My dear, frenzied friend—
How I ache for her, Lord.
I just can't believe
How busy she is.

She eats so fast
Scolds so loudly
Clings so tightly
Complains so bitterly
Worries so intensely
Rushes so wildly
Shops so impulsively
Plans so fearfully
Panics so frequently
Shatters so utterly

No wonder she insists
There's no time to pray.

With deep repose
Until that bright and shining dawn
When You shall say
"You're home."

The First Time I Held You

As you are placed in my arms
I must tell you now
I've never been in such awe
Of the One who ordained life.
I keep thinking, "What have I done
To deserve this precious baby?"
God gently whispers back
"It's a gift."

I try to hold back the tears
Knowing He has entrusted to my care
One He loved enough to die for.
I'm overwhelmed, knowing I am inadequate
For this incredible task.
"Depend on Me, count on My grace"
I hear Him say so clearly.

As I gaze upon you, my newborn child
I am engulfed in His love, so aware
He gave His only Son for me, for you.
Then joyfully I hear His words:
"I love you."

I'm sure I never really understood
His love for me quite as I do today.
The day I received you—my child
My reward, my gift from God.
I thought you'd like to know what I felt
The first time I held you in my arms.

Lady in Pink

Lord, it happened so unexpectedly
That October Sunday.
I caught a glimpse of her
Starting slowly down the aisle—
Silver hair
Pink shawl hugging her tiny frame.
Your prompting was inescapable . . .
"Take her home for dinner."
Her eyes glistened with surprise:
"Nobody's invited me to dinner
Since Charlie died."

Lord, it was a rewarding Sunday.
She was like a happy child
Celebrating Christmas. . . .
We talked about Charlie
About knitting and painting
About peach preserves
And the goodness of God.
Our home was charged with love—
With laughter.

A Life
of Wisdom

Part of the Gift

I heard today
Of a decrepit native woma
Who walked mile after mile
Under the blistering sun
To bring a small gift of embroide
To the missionary she deeply loved.
Hour after hour she trudged
Over rough, rugged roads
Clutching tightly her small gift.
Her weary body sagged
Her vision blurred
Her bare feet bled from the jagged rocks.

Grateful but overwhelmed
The missionary wept.
The trembling old woman spoke softly:
"Please understand.
The walk is part of the gift."

My Lord
My commitment to You is for life.
I give myself to You unreservedly
To do with me as You please.
But may I not forget
That the tears, the fears
The strain and the pain

Relentless

God, You are relentless.
I have yielded
Everything to You—
Everything but one small exception—
An exception so small
I'm truly amazed
You would even take notice.
Yet it is invariably
To that one small exception
That You keep bringing me
Back, and back, and back.
Why does it matter so much to You?

My child
Why does it matter so much to you?

The Great Stirring

O God
I know You are determined
That I shall not become careless
In my attitude toward You.
You know how easily I am lulled
Into sleepy satisfaction with myself.
I'm prone to think that nobody really knows
Quite as well as I what is best for me—
Not even You, God!

There is a secret inclination to say
"I'll call You when I need you
And in the meantime please bless me."
Then when I am not in the least prepared
There comes a great stirring up
Of my entire being and I am amazed to see
How totally unqualified I am to direct
And to manage my own life.

I Wonder

You know, Lord, how I serve You
With great emotional fervor
In the limelight.
You know how eagerly I speak for You
At a women's club.
You know how I effervesce when I promote
A fellowship group.
You know my genuine enthusiasm
At a Bible study.

But how would I react, I wonder
If You pointed to a basin of water
And asked me to wash the calloused feet
Of a bent and wrinkled old woman
Day after day
Month after month
In a room where nobody saw
And nobody knew.

Lost Argument

I read this morning
Your direct and piercing question
To the ancient Job:
"Do you still want to argue
With the Almighty?
Or will you yield?"
With thoughtful heart
I read Job's wise reply:
"I am nothing. . . .
How could I find the answers?
I lay my hand upon my mouth in silence."
You know so well what I do, God.
I continue to argue with You
As though I were in charge.
As though I could solve my own dilemma.
Finally in the end, broken and defeated
I yield to You, and then—peace.
Forgive me, dear God
For so foolishly ending
Where I should have begun.

The Deliberate No

O God, teach me to say
The deliberate and releasing word *no*
Without a spiritual tug-of-war
Between variations of false guilt.
May I say it tactfully
Kindly and gently
But enable me to *say* it!
If on occasions I am forced
To confront an honest doubt
May I wait patiently
For Your clear guidance.
May this powerful truth
Penetrate the inner chambers of my being:
It is better to say a God-guided no
Than a self-guided yes.
Lord, remind me often
That a squirrel cage
Can be mighty confining.
So can a heart attack
And a hospital bed.

How eagerly I would do
In seven short days
What You've persistently pressed upon me
For the past several months.
Lord, is it too late?

"And they immediately . . . followed him."
(Matthew 4:20)

For this we both know:
To sacrifice the ultimate

For the immediate
Spells disaster
Despair
Defeat.

A Quiet Tongue

Lord, a revealing fact
Began to surface today:
I talk more than I listen.
I seem to be thoroughly convinced
That my ideas
My inspiring experiences
My bits of wisdom
Are exactly what all my friends need.
Too often I break into conversations
Confident that my enlightened insight
Will solve the predicament—
Whatever it is.
Obviously, I feel more comfortable
When I'm expounding.

But this morning at a Bible study
I cringed when I read Your command
In the first chapter of James:
"Don't ever forget
That it is best to listen much
Speak little, and not become angry."
At first I wanted to run.
But as the words kept battering away
At my guilty heart
I finally circled them with red ink.
Now, Lord, please help me to obey them.
Remind me daily, hourly
That listening is a discipline
And a discipline always costs.

Phone Call

I answered the phone
And I wished I hadn't.
Lord, she keeps talking and talking
And there's no way to stop her.
She asks a question
And gives her own answer.
In the middle of one story
She starts another.
Today she said lustily:
"Life is just rush rush rush."
I prayed that she'd rush
To her kitchen.

Lord, when she calls I feel trapped—
Pushed into a corner.
I want to say, "No, no
I haven't the time today."
Yet when I think of Your patience
I am gnawed by guilt.
Is it a false guilt, Lord?
I honestly think my emotions
Are more harmed
Than hers are helped.
Am I wrong?

Tell me, please tell me . . .
How would *You* handle such calls?

Forgive My Critical Attitude

Lord
Forgive my critical attitude—
My judgmental spirit.
It is true that I saw my friend fall again
But not once did I consider
The countless times she did *not* fall
Though she was severely tempted.
Help me to bind myself more closely
And more lovingly to her.
May she know that I continue to believe
In Your victory in her life
Despite any sudden barrier of defeat.
May I redouble my love and vigilance
Until she is renewed and restored—
Until she is able to give to others
The support she herself has received.

I Keep Running Back to You

You know how it is with me, Lord:
So often I mess up my days.
I judge harshly
I am critical and obstinate
I waste time and energy
I blame others for my failure.
There are people I try to avoid
And tasks I try to evade
And when I can't have my own way
I sulk in my own little corner.
Lord, I even turn my back on You
To escape Your penetrating gaze.

Then finally I get fed up with myself.
The intolerable loneliness frightens me
And I can no longer endure my shame.
It always happens, Lord—
I keep running back to You!

Where else can I go?
Who else understands me so well
Or forgives me so totally?
Who else can save me from foolish pride?
No one, Lord, but You.
So thank You for accepting me
For loving me
For always welcoming me.
I just can't help it, Lord
I keep running back to You!

Never Too Late

Sometimes, dear Lord
You work so slowly!

*Tell Me, dear child
Have I ever been too late?*

Burning Bushes

O God
I come to You penitently j
Confessing I have spent
Far too many hours
Exploring the dramatic
The ecstatic, the sensational.
I have been much too engrossed
In looking for burning bushes.
All the while
You have been waiting for me
To take off my shoes
Bow before You
And crown You LORD of my life.

Moment by Moment

Today, dear Lord
I asked You how I could know
If my surrender was complete.
I asked if I had truly yielded
All that I am and all that I have.
Simply but directly You answered
"How is it with you now, this moment?
Settle it each moment
And you won't need to ask."

Immediately

Dear Lord
I'm so tired of living
In my little cramped vessel—
So weary of dangling my feet in the water
But never stepping out of the boat.
I want to walk the waves with You
Just as Peter did.
True, he took only a few steps
Before losing his courage
But at least he was heading toward You.
Lord, I'm coming, too!
If I begin to falter or sink
I trust You to catch me
Just as You caught Peter.
Remember, Lord?
You caught him *immediately*.

Small Bit of Heaven

Make me, dear Lord
A small bit of Heaven
In a sick and frenzied world
So seemingly intent
On destroying itself.

The Time Is Now

Lord
I see with startling clarity
That life is never long enough
To put You off
Until tomorrow.
The things that are before
Are all too soon behind.
I can never pick up
The years I've put down.
If I intend
To walk with You tomorrow
I must start today.

Loving Me As You Do

When my rapport with You
Is disturbed, Lord
My rapport with myself
Is utterly destroyed.

I am irritable
Little things get in my way
I am short with my family
The house is too small
My neighbors bore me
The phone frustrates me
Feelings of guilt gnaw at me.
Just leave me alone, I scream
I'll do it myself.

But You patiently wait to be gracious.
You gently nudge me to attention.
For knowing me as You do
Loving me as You do
You understand so well
That when I want You least
I need You most.

Make Me Faithful, Lord

Lord, it has become very clear to me
That faithfulness is clearly measurable.
It is, in fact, easily detected
Not only by me, but by those who know me.

Either I keep my promise to get up
When the alarm sounds
Or I cover my head with my pillow
And sleep another hour or so.
Either I am on time for an appointment
Or I inconvenience others by being late.

I spend quality time with You alone
Or I fill my days with trivialities
Making excuses that are weak and lame.
I write the three letters I owe
Or I push them away for another day.
I make the call I promised to make
Or I rationalize
I'm really too tired to talk now.
I pay the pledge I made for a worthy cause
Or I purchase the new shoes I didn't need.
I follow You with my whole heart
Or I take halfway measures
And plead for Your forgiveness.

A Life
through Darkness

In the Darkness

O my Lord
I am slowly beginning to see
That I must *listen* to You
In the darkness
Instead of desperately
Pleading for light.
I am beginning to sense
That darkness is not always
An indication of my failure
Or of Your displeasure.
Rather it is an indication
Of Your outstretched arms
Waiting to hold me
Close, close to Your heart.
Darkness, which so often
Seems to be a reason
For fear and despair
May be in Your plan, dear God
A source of deep purification.

Heartstrings

Lord, with no sense of direction
I'm forever losing my way.
Please tie a string
From Your heart to mine
So that even in the darkness
I'll feel the tug of Your heart
And find my way home.

But what do you think happ...
God Himself calmed my quiv...
He removed all the barriers
Erected by my self-indulgence
He forgave me completely.
Then with incredible gentleness
He whispered . . .
"Had you asked
I would have carried you
All the way!"

I Know You Best

God
So often I have
Seen and heard You
Between smiles
And singing
And laughter.
But I am beginning to see
I learn to know You best
Between sobs.

I Trust

O God, thank You
That Your promises are valid
As long as the world lasts.
They do not suddenly dissolve
When my faith is feeble
And my courage fails.
When You have given a promise
You will perform it—
Sight or no sight
Feeling or no feeling.

You may take me
Through the darkest night
The deepest waters.
The very worst may happen
But out of it
You will bring the very best
For Your Word remains secure.

Lord, keep me faithful in my trust.
When I can articulate no other prayer
May my waiting heart
Continually avow:
I trust!
I trust!

I Plead with You

Lord of my longing heart
I plead with You
To help me want *You*
More than I want *this*.
The unquenchable desire within
Is so overpowering, so consuming
At times I think
I can no longer endure it.
I think I would rather die
Than live without
That which so completely absorbs me.
And yet, dear God
There is the unwavering conviction
That what I want
Is not what You want for me.
There is the deep certainty
That the day would come
When my personal choice
Would close every future open door.
Lord, I cannot handle this alone.
I am not strong enough
Nor am I willing enough.
You alone can change my heart's desire.
You alone can make all things new.
O dear Lord, please help me
To want *You* more than I want *this*.

Above all
Thank You for saying no
When in anguish I asked
"If I give You all else
May I keep *this?*"

Lord, my awe increases
When I see the wisdom
Of Your divine no.

Limping Home

Lord
With a crooked stick for a cane
I'm limping home.
Mocked and maligned
Stooped and stupid
Soiled and shabby
I limp toward You.
You could say, "I told you so."
You could say, "It's a little too late."
You could say, "Wait while I think it over."
You could sweep me under the rug—
We both know I deserve far less.
But when I see the Cross
And the Man who died there
Suddenly I know I limp
Toward unfathomable love
And there is forgiveness
Rushing toward me.
I don't ask for a banquet, Lord
Nor do I need a gold ring.
I'm so hungry
So thirsty
For You.

The Majestic Name

My hospital room
Is just a few feet from the elevator.
Third floor. Room 322.
Over and over I hear the monotonous hum
Of the sliding doors.
Open, shut . . . open, shut . . .

A white rubberized curtain separates me
From the fragile, gray-haired woman
In the bed next to mine.
I hear her frustrated sigh
As she constantly attempts
To find a comfortable position.
She is in obvious pain.

My own pain is so agonizing
My mind so steeped in darkness
I can neither read nor pray.
The smallest thing becomes a herculean
    effort—
Like pulling the sheet over my shoulder.
Like sipping water from a straw.
I feel helpless, just so utterly helpless.

But one thing I can do, dear Lord.
I can repeat the powerful Name of Jesus.
Again and again I say it:
Jesus . . .
Jesus . . .

A Doubt

Sometimes, dear Lord
You don't seem
To love me at all.

Sometimes, dear child
You seem to ignore
The eternal facts.

Child of My love
In My infinite Plan
There are four seasons.
Trust Me . . . Trust Me. . . .
I promise you—Spring.

Listen Trustingly

Lord, I'm listening.
Why don't I hear You?

Fretful child
You listen
Strenuously
Anxiously
Laboriously.

Rest in Me
And listen
Trustingly.
I am talking
All the time.

My child
Because I love you so much
I wait for you to let Me
Remove the harmful desire.

Beginning

Lord
I'm at the end
Of all my resources.

Child
You're just at the beginning
Of Mine.

Help us, God. Please help us.
We really love each other
But we've been in nursery school
Much too long!

When I Cannot Utter a Word

Because of a strange chemical imbalance
My husband had lost his ability to speak.
He could hear me
He could understand me
But despite his longing desire
He could not verbally respond.
The doctor assured me
The puzzling malady would pass.
However, he was not sure how soon.
I sat by the hospital bed
Watching and waiting
Fervently praying.
I held my husband's hand.
Gently, ever so gently
I told him of my love.
Through the long, difficult hours
I continually reassured him.
He heard me, I knew he heard me.
In his tired eyes I saw his love.
But he could not utter a word . . .
Not a single word.

Why?

I'm singing today
In the midst of adversity—
Singing without reason for song.
Lord, do You want to know why?
Simply because I'm staunchly convinced
That as I continue my songs in the night
You'll create a new reason for singing.

Romans 8–To Me

God
I may fall flat on my face
I may fail until I feel
Old and beaten and done in
Yet Your love for me is changeless.
All the music may go out of my life
My private world may shatter to dust
Even so You will hold me
In the palm of Your steady hand.
No turn in the affairs
Of my fractured life
Can baffle You.
Satan with all his braggadocio
Cannot distract You.
Nothing can separate me
From Your measureless love:
Pain can't
Disappointment can't
Anguish can't.
Yesterday, today, tomorrow can't.
The loss of my dearest love can't.

I Sing in the Rain

One cold, misty day
When I was nine years old
I walked hand in hand
Through a wooded forest
With my strong, gentle father.
"Listen to the stillness," he whispered.
"Stillness makes beautiful music."
Suddenly he pointed to a tiny bird
Perched on a limb of a bending tree.
"The bird doesn't know we're here
But he's singing his heart out."
Then smiling down at me he asked
"Could you sing in the rain
If nobody heard you but God?"

Lord, though many years have passed
Since I walked with my father
I have never forgotten his question.
Today I am alone—
Yet not alone, for YOU are here.
Though my heart is grief-drenched
I know You are worthy of praise.
Help me, please help me
To sing my feeble song in the rain
Though nobody hears but You.

Confession

Our family remembers . . .
When my sister
Was a very little girl
She stood in the middle
Of our living room
Stamped her foot
With little-girl authority
And publicly announced to all five of us
"I'm so tired of being good!"

Today while I was hurriedly trying
To tackle a hundred unfinished tasks
Smudged blue jeans
Hair a total mess
I stood in the middle of our kitchen
Pushing away thoughts of former freedom
And silently screamed for only myself
"I'm so tired of being good!"

I'm a Slow Learner, Lord

Lord, I'm sure I see
The reason for my confusion
More clearly today
Than I did six months ago
When the loss was still so painful.
And now as you ask me
To face with poise and serenity
Whatever detachments You require of me
I trust I'm beginning to sense
That whatever You permit
Of deprivation and isolation
Has infinite meaning—
Far beyond my present capacity to
    understand.
But I'm a slow learner, Lord.
May I ask You to teach me
How to develop poise and serenity?
I long so much to please You
But even this I cannot do without
The assurance of Your promised help.

A Life
of Joy

It Keeps Happening

Dear Lord
When You came into my life
With Your immeasurable love
And liberating power
Something wonderful happened.
Day after day
Year after year
It keeps happening . . .
And happening . . .
And happening. . . .

Will You Walk with Me?

Lord, I love this fresh April morning!
The sky is brilliantly blue.
Shiny fresh buds are forming
On the trees in our parkway.
Lord, will You walk with me today
As You've done so often before?

You've walked with me
Over rough and dangerous roads . . .
Over narrow, winding paths.
When my heart was wrapped in darkness
You've walked with me
Through miles of parched wilderness.
You've walked with me
Through emotional earthquakes
Which uprooted my total being.

But Lord, if You'll walk with me today
I'm confident You'll discover
That my faith has quietly grown.
I'm no longer so frenzied and fearful.
Our walks have changed me completely.
Never once did You leave my side.

On this fresh spring morning
My heart overflows with one desire:
As we walk I want to praise
The Majesty and the Splendor of You.
Will You walk with me, Lord?

You Said to Me Today

My Lord
You said to me today
*"With everlasting kindness
I will have compassion on you."*

You said to me today
*"I am with you
And will watch over you
Wherever you go."*

You said to me today
*"Do not be afraid.
Stand firm and you will see
The deliverance of the Lord."*

You said to me today
*"Commit to the Lord
Whatever you do
And your plans will succeed."*

You said to me today
*"Those who hope in the Lord
Will renew their strength."*

You said to me today
*"The eyes of the Lord
Are on those who fear him
On those who hope
In his unfailing love."*

My Life Is Richer

How can I thank her, dear Lord
For what she did for me today?
How can I express my sudden release
Because she genuinely cared?
It was such a simple gesture, really—
A friendship card with a single line:
"My life is richer because of you."

You know, Lord, how numb I felt
Before the mail arrived.
Morning came much too soon
And I awakened weary, depleted.
For some unaccountable reason
Our house looked dismal and drab.
Most of the morning I berated myself
And fought a losing battle with doubt.
Then I heard the mailman.

O God, is it really true?
Is someone's life richer because of me?
Despite my whimpering
My defeats, my petty concerns
Am I usable in Your Kingdom, after all?
Suddenly, God, I believe that I am!

Forgive me for wasting a glorious morning
That should have been wrapped in praise.
Thank You especially for the friend
Who gathered my scattered emotions
And fused them into serenity

Yellow Cat

Almost every evening a yellow cat
Finds his personal place
On a comfortable lounge chair
On our patio.
He has no doubt I shall be privileged
To welcome him with open arms
When I unlock our back door
First thing in the morning.

Every morning I clap my hands
Hoping the yellow cat will understand
I am urging him to move on.
He stays!

When a more forceful clap
Makes the message clear
He casually heads toward other patios
To wait with monarch patience
For an engraved invitation.

What a way to live—unless deep inside
The yellow cat really believes
He has a claim to a whole city block.
Somehow he seems to sense
That God made yellow cats
And he is grateful to be a part
Of God's wonderful world
Where there are patios
And comfortable lounge chairs.

New Bible

This was an exciting day for me, Lord!
This morning I opened my new Bible.
Not a single word was circled
Not a single phrase underlined.
Now with each new day
I can circle and underline again
I can word-clutter the margins
And I know what will happen, Lord—
I'll be asking as I read
Why didn't I see that before?
But even with the joy of a new Bible
I'm going to miss my old one
With its tattered pages—
Its creased and torn edges.
Oh, how many personal notes
Are jotted on the margins
How many God-whispered secrets.
Yes, Lord, I'll miss it.
But thank You for a friend's reminder:
"If your Bible is falling apart
Chances are your life isn't."

Spiritual Mathematics

Lord
Today I suddenly remember
Something my father said years ago
As we sat at our dinner table
When we were children:
"If I have a dollar
And you have a dollar
And we exchange those dollars
We still each have one dollar.
But if I have a thought
And you have a thought
And we exchange those thoughts
We each have two thoughts."

Several hours from now, Lord
I'll be eating lunch
With a group of very special women.
We'll be expressing ideas
Sharing concepts
Exchanging thoughts.
O God, give us, I pray
The mind of Christ.
May His expressed thoughts through us
Multiply a thousand times
And leave indelible impressions
Of Your magnificent love.

Thank You so much, dear God
For the certain knowledge that Jesus
(Who always obeyed the Father)
Went apart from the crowd to rest.
So must I!

Moving Day

Lord
Day after day
For twenty years
I joyfully thanked You
For our family of six
Living harmoniously
In our comfortable home.
Today, dear Lord
I joyfully thank You
For our family of five
And for a thousand
Beautiful memories
Of one who so quietly moved
To the home You prepared
And now lives in splendor
With You.

Autumn Glow

Lord, if You will make
The autumn of my life
As lovely as this
Golden autumn morning
I will not look back to grieve
The passing days of summer.
Of all the regal seasons
Autumn is most brilliant.
Make my life brilliant, too!

Marvelous Moments

What a beautiful relief, dear God
To sit quietly in my own living room
Soaking up the luxury of aloneness.
No demanding voices
No radio or television
No shouts from the bathroom
Just these few marvelous moments
To kick off my shoes
Shed my confusion
And reclaim myself . . .
These few marvelous moments
To respond to Your persistent plea
"Be still and know that I am God."

So thank You again and again
For ten thousand "coincidences"
Always in the nick of time
When I pray.

Accept—Expect

My Father
Empower me to *accept*
All You have promised
And to *expect*
Every promise fulfilled.
May I never forget
How completely I am in Your hands.

A Favorite Gift

There was that day my husband
Came home with an apple corer for me—
His idea of a wonderful surprise.
Somehow, he just couldn't fathom
My going through all of life
Without an apple corer.
Now an apple corer takes apples
And there I was with my shiny new gadget
And not an apple in the house.
It often happens that way—
One thing calls for another.
We dashed to the store and came home
With the biggest apples we could find.
We had ourselves a coring party
To surpass all parties.
Then for a solid week we ate baked apples.
Funny thing about that corer—
After all these years I still have it
And it's one of my favorite gifts.

When You gave her Ryan, Kyle, Karis, and
   Megan—
Her four unmerited favors from You?
Did You really know, dear Lord?

A Personal Psalm

There is no place I can go
Where You are not.
There is no hiding from You
For always and forever
You have already found me.
If I fly fast and high
Through clouds and sky
You meet and greet me.
If I plunge into depths, valleys
Oceans and canyons
You catch me, hold me, lift me.
When depression overcomes me
And fear pierces my heart
You pulse Your love through me
And again I throb with life.
When I put my blinders on
Escaping into darkened thought
You touch me with a ray of light
And free me from the mask I wear.
There is no black, there is no white
There is no day, there is no night
All is color, glorious and bright
For You are always with me
Holding me . . . holding me tight.